The Toronto Protocol

The real plan of the Global Elite?

Corstown – MMXII

© Brian Nugent, Co. Meath, 2011-12.
ISBN 978-1-4710-7002-0
Anybody is free to copy this text around for any purposes whatsoever short of a full book of the text sold for serious commercial purposes. Also the French orginal, on which this is based, is of course not the copyright of this writer.

CONTENTS

Preface..4

Introduction, by Serge Monast..6

"Bread and Circuses," the 1967 document..........................8

"The Red Dawn," the 1985 document................................18

Conclusion, by Serge Monast..28

PREFACE

This is a translation from the French of a document compiled by a clique of senior financiers who met in Canada in 1967 and then in 1985. Its a pretty explosive paper which documents a far reaching conspiracy to set up a global government by means of corrupting the people and finances of nation states, and much else besides. I think its extremely interesting but there is no doubt that most people will shake their heads in wonder that a group like this could really exist.

It comes to us via an investigative journalist in Canada called Serge Monast, quite a well known and respected figure whom you can see give a lecture in French in the image on the back cover and on video here: http://www.youtube.com/watch?v=m-hn4OiJKSA.

He was also responsible for leaking the better known "Operation Blue Beam" document, which you can read in numerous places on the net. We are told that he had various sources from which he got his information:

> "It is true that it was informed by repented politicians, and disgusted Secret Service agents. He also received classified, ultra confidential, documents, often anonymously or transmitted by fellow-members [of the International Free Press] located at the four corners of the world."

It has also been said that this particular document originated from French intelligence. (Monast was from French speaking Canada.)

In any case this really is a remarkable account and Monast himself concluded that it is up to each individual reader to make their own mind up on whether to believe this document, by, he recommends, seeing if it matches the politics, and recent political history, of the last few years.

It seems to this observer that there are many such documents floating around the internet and of course its up to each individual to make their minds up as to what is authentic and what isn't, but sometimes you can be struck by the cleverness and deep thinking in a given paper which might cause you to dismiss the idea that it was just a forgery. That I think is what this document does and that is why I place before the general public this short pamphlet of it, the first translation of the document into English from the French text that Serge Monast leaked in March 1995.

Brian Nugent
Co Meath, Ireland, January 2012

INTRODUCTION
by Serge Monast

"End of June 1967: in Montreal there is Expo 67; in Ottawa, there are the final preparations for the "Centenary of the Confederation"; in the U.S. it is the challenge of the Vietnam War and, through the country, the "Flower Power". We are close to the events of May '68 in France, the explosion of nationalism in Quebec, the Woodstock Festival in the U.S. ... but at the same time, the end of June 1967 marks the final preparations for the development of the Plan of the "Fall of Nations" by the highest levels of Anglo-Saxon Freemasonry in Toronto (Canada).

This secret meeting, highly "Confidential", is organized by the "6.6.6", (so they call themselves), i.e. those who run the 6 largest banks in the world, the 6 largest energy consortia on the planet (including the oil part), and the 6 largest consortia of agri-food (which includes the control of the principal routes in the food world ["principales routes alimentaires du monde"]).

These 6.6.6., being the most senior international financiers, will define, within their meeting, a "Common Strategy" for absolute control over "World Trade"; on the possession of the Energy Weapon (the gateway of the twenty-first century ["porte ouverte sur le XXIe siècle"]); and the international control of the food (which also includes, for them, the pharmaceutical companies which include, in turn, the global market for "Vitamins" and "vaccines").

Their "plan" boils down to three major themes: "The Economic, the Political, and the Social Policy for the 70s and 80s. If successful, it must inevitably lead to the capture of "Global Power" by implementing the "New World Order", the same which U.S. President George Bush will do much to promote in the early 90s.

The Title of the Document of the 6.6.6.: "PANEM and circuses" (From Bread and Circus Games) [i.e. an old Roman phrase to describe how the Emperors used to entertain and feed the masses so that they would be distracted from taking an interest in politics.].

The Goal of the Globalist Project: The "Genocide of the Vital for the Benefit and Profit of the Occult. ["Génocide du Vital au Profit du Rentable Occulte"]"

Means of Financing the Project: Among other things, use of Humanitarian Aid, and of Food Aid International to finance the "Multinationals" of the 6.6.6.

THE DOCUMENT:

[This concludes what Monast was saying and what follows is the actual document.]

CHAPTER 1
"Bread and Circuses," the 1967 document

All historical periods that led to the decline of civilizations were all marked, without exception, by "the spirit of errancy of men". Today, we must ensure that that "Spirit" will result from a "World Society of Leisure" in all its forms. This "Leisure" should consist of [Sex, (these five square brackets are by Monast)], [drugs], [Sport], the [Exotic Travel] and [Entertainment] in general, but accessible to all strata of society. Man must come to believe that it is "Modern", and that modernity consists of its present capacity and, possibility, to enjoy greatly everything that surrounds it.

To achieve this objective it is imperative to be able to infiltrate the Media (Radio, TV, Newspapers), the milieu of the "Mode" and "Culture" (the milieu of the New Music) by which we will influence, for sure, all sections of Western societies. So taking under our thumb the "Sense" of young people (the adults of tomorrow), we will therefore open the way to infiltrate and transform profoundly, without arousing suspicion, Politics, the Legal System and Education, which will allow us to fundamentally change the course, the future direction of, Society envisaged by our "Plan".

The people we know, have not historical memory. They tirelessly repeat the mistakes of the past without realizing that these errors had led their fathers before them into the same descent as they will live in, only worse, before the end of this century. See, for example, how their grandfathers have lived at the beginning of this century, thanks to the hard work of our predecessors.

Having known, without limits, the release of morals, and the abolition of morality (in other words, the errancy of the spirit), they experienced the "Economic Crisis" and the "War." Today their grandchildren and their children are heading towards a similar conclusion, even worse, because this time we will finally establish our "New World Order" and none of them are able of realizing it, they will all be too preoccupied in meeting their overly sensual needs, the very basic.

A "Norm" generally very important, which has already proven itself at the beginning of this century in the construction and the establishment of the [Communist system] by the late Senior officers of our Lodges, is the profitability of the "Exception". In principle, we know that, the exception proves the general rule is contrary to it. But in our vocabulary, the Exception is what must be imposed on all. We need to make "Exceptions", in different spheres of society, the new "Rules" generally applicable to all, a primary objective of all future social protests led by the Youth of Nations.

Thus the Exception will be the detonator by which all the historical society will collapse on itself in shortness of breath and unprecedented confusion.

The foundation of "Western Society", in essence, comes straight from the Judeo-Christian heritage. Precisely the same legacy that made the "Family", the "Node", and the "Cornerstone" of all the current social structure. Our predecessors who had financed the revolutionary writers of the late nineteenth century and early twentieth century had understood the importance of splitting, then to break, this "vital core" if they wanted in Russia to achieve the new "Communist system" of the time.

And that is precisely what they did by carefully producing by philosophers and writers, nonconformists of the time,: "A Manifesto for the glory of the God-state [the State as God]"; which has the absolute primacy over the individual, over the "Family".

To succeed with certainty to the construction of a World Government, [A New World Order Community] where all individuals without exception, will be subject to the "World State" of the "New Order", we must, first, remove the "Family" (which will, in turn, lead to the loss of ancestral religious teachings), and secondly, levelling all individuals by removing the "Social Classes", in particular, the "Middle Classes". But we must proceed so that all these are seen as being from the popular will, that they have the appearance of "Democracy".

Using isolated cases, but amplifying them to the extreme using student protests infiltrated by us, journalists sympathetic to our cause and purchased politicians, we will be able to establish new bodies that have every appearance of "Modernity", such as an "Office for the Protection of Children", protected by a "Charter of Rights and Freedoms".

For the success of our "Global Plan: [The Red Plan]", we need to implement in all societies of the West in the 70s, an "Office for Protection of Children" where staff (young intellectuals with no experience, fresh out of universities which highlighted our internationalist principles) will follow to the letter, without discernment, the "Charter of the Rights of the Child". Who would dare oppose it without at the same time being labelled as barbarians from the Middle Ages?

In the "Charter", laboriously developed in our "Lodges", we will finally wipe out any parental authority by breaking the family into people fiercely opposed to each other to protect their interests. It will encourage children to report parents who are too authoritarian as being too traditional, too religious. It will thus contribute to subject parents to a "Collective Psychosis of Fear"; this will inevitably give rise, generally in society, to a relaxation of parental authority. Thus we will have succeeded, initially, to produce a society like that of Russia in the 50s where children denounced their parents to the state, and this without anyone noticing.

In thus transferring to the State the "Parental Role", it will be easier, then, for us to grab, one by one, all the responsibilities that had been, to date, the sole responsibility of the parents. So that we can have it considered by all as an abuse against the child, religious instruction of traditional Judeo-Christian origin.

At the same time but at another level, we will include in the highest Laws of Nations, that all Religions, Cults and religious Practices of all kinds, including "Sorcery and Magic", must all be met in the same way as each other.

It will be profitable later to transfer the role of the State in relation to the child to the highest international bodies, such as the United Nations.

Understand this well: "Our goal is not to protect children, or anyone from another, but to cause the collapse and subsequent fall of Nations which are a major obstacle to the implementation of our "New World Order." That is why the "Office of Child Protection" must be invested with absolute legal authority. They must be able, as they see fit, but always under the pretext of protecting the child, to remove them from their original home environments and place them in family backgrounds or foreign government centres that have been established for our internationalist principles and religions. Therefore, it will complete the final breaking of the "Western Family Unit". For without the protection and monitoring of their original parents, these children will be permanently handicapped in their psychological and moral development, and consequently represent natural prey, easily adaptable to our global aspirations.

For success to be achieved by such an enterprise, it is essential that staff working in these 'Offices" in the service of the state, are young people without experience, imbued with theories that we know are empty and ineffectual, and especially, are obsessed with the missionary spirit as great protectors of children at risk. For them, all parents must represent potential criminals, potential hazards to the welfare of the child, here considered a "God."

An "Office of Child Protection" and a "Charter of the Rights of the Child" have no reason to be without children at risk [i.e. there can be real examples to justify them]. In addition, exceptions and the historical examples used in their [i.e. the Office and the Charter] creation would sooner or later disappear if they were not constantly fed with new cases occurring on an ongoing basis. In this sense, we must infiltrate the "Education System" of Nations to make disappear, under the cover of "Modernity" and "Evolution", the teaching of Religion, of History, and Good Manners, while diluting at the same time, under an avalanche of new experiments in the milieu of Education, that of language and mathematics.

In this way, by depriving the younger generations any grounding in and any frontier to morals, any knowledge of the past (and therefore any national pride), all respect for others, power through knowledge of language and science (and thus of the reality), we will help build a youth largely prepared for all forms of delinquency. In this new world fragmented by fear of parents, and their abandonment of any responsibility for their children, we will open the way to train in our own way and according to our primary objectives, a youth where arrogance, contempt, and humiliation of others, will be considered as the new basis of "Affirmation of Self" and "Freedom".

But we know, from similar past experiences, that such a youth is already doomed to its own destruction because it is inherently "individualist", so "Anarchist" by definition. In this sense, it cannot possibly represent a solid basis for the continuity of any society whatsoever, much less a safe bet for the care of its elderly.

In the same vein, it is equally imperative to create a "Charter of Rights and Individual Freedoms" and "Office of the Protection of the Citizen" with the promise to the masses that these innovations are part and parcel of "Modernity" and of the "New Society" of the twentieth century.

Similarly, at the same time, but at another level, to pass new laws for the "Respect of Individual Liberty". As in the case of the "Family", but under the plan for the "Society", these laws will conflict with the Rights of the Community, leading for the societies involved, their right to self-destruction. For here, the reversal is complete: "It's not the society (the right of the majority) to be protected against people who may threaten, but rather (the Right of the Individual) which is to be protected against potential threats from the majority." That's the goal we set ourselves.

To complete the breakup of the family, and of the education system, therefore the Society in general, it is essential to encourage "Sexual Freedom" at all levels of Western Society. We must reduce the individual, and so the masses, to an obsession with satisfying their primary instincts by all possible means. We know that this step represents the culmination by which any society will collapse on itself. Was it not so when the Roman Empire [fell] from its apogee, like all civilizations throughout history?

By men of science and laboratories funded by our Lodges, we were able to develop a chemical process that will revolutionize all Western Societies, and relegate to oblivion forever, moral principles and the Judeo-Christian religion. This process, in pill form, will open the door wide to "Sexual Freedom" without consequences, and push the "Women" of Nations to want to break with what will be seen as the yoke of the past (the slavery, women subject to men and the traditional Judeo-Christian family).

Formerly the "Centre and pivot of the family unit," the modern woman, now as an independent, wants to break with its traditional role, separate from the family and live her life according to her own personal aspirations. Nothing more natural, we know, but where we will intervene strongly [is in] infiltrating all new "Women's Movements", and accordingly push their logic to its extreme limits. And these limits are already written down as the final breakdown of the traditional family and Judeo-Christian Society.

This "Sexual Liberation" is the ultimate means by which we will be able to get rid out of the "Conscience of the People" a reference to "Good and Evil". The collapse of the moral and religious barriers will allow us to complete the process of the false "Liberation of Man from his Past", but which in reality is a form of slavery that will benefit our "Globalist Plans".

The door opened for the encouragement of "sexual Liberty", to "Divorce", to "Abortion" on demand, to various forms of legal recognition of homosexuality, will help us to fundamentally alter the historical basis of the "Legal Rights" of Societies. It will be a major push on all individuals towards a general loosening of morals, to divide people against each other, according to their instincts and their own interests, to destroy the future of the youth, pushing for damaging experiences of early sexuality and abortion, and to break the morality of future generations by pushing them to alcoholism, drugs of any kind (with respect to which our Senior Officers of the International Lodges will take care to take over the world) and suicide (the latter considered by disenchanted youths, abandoned and left to themselves, as a chivalrous end).

Lets disappoint the Nation's youth by showing them to their parents as irresponsible, irreligious, immoral, not ambitious, giving themselves over to pleasure, escape, and unbridled satisfaction of their instincts, at the cost of lies, hypocrisy and betrayal. Let's make divorce and abortion socially acceptable.

Let's push it and crime in all its forms, and then they will take refuge in separate groups, out of reach of the home environment, which will change, inevitably, because of the threat to its survival. The social fabric is disrupted and forever, we will then be able to act on the Politics and Economy of Nations, to submit them to our mercy, and they will come to accept by force, our plans for a New Order World.

For, it must be confessed, that Nations which cannot count on a strong youth, a society where individuals are grouped around a common ideal, reinforced with walls of unwavering morals, which, historically, would have been able to provide support, can not abdicate our global commitment.

So then we can inaugurate what was announced by both our past creations: "The communist system who prophesied a world revolution set in motion by all the rejects of the earth", and "Nazism in which we had announced a New World Order for 1000 years". That is our ultimate goal, the award of the work of all the brave fallen for the performance of this work over the centuries. Say it loud and clear: "All the Brothers of the past Lodges, who died in anonymity for the realization of this ideal that we are now able to touch with the tips of our fingers."

It is generally acknowledged that Man, once having secured his basic needs (food, clothing and shelter), is much more likely to be less vigilant. Let us allow him to lull his conscience, while we direct our own thing in his mind ["tout en orientant à notre guise son esprit en lui créant"], by creating favourable economic conditions. So, during this period of the 70s where our agents will slip across the different spheres of Society to accept our new standards in Education, Legal Rights, and Social Policy, we will spread it around in a confident economic climate.

Work for all; the opening of Credit for all; Recreation for all, will work tandem to create an illusion of a new social class: the "Middle Class". Because once we have achieved our goals, this "class" in the middle, between the secular poor, and us rich, will definitely disappear by cutting off all means of survival.

In this sense, we will make the Nation-States the new "Parents" of individuals. Through this climate of confidence, which our "International Agents" will act to reinforce by removing any spectre of world war, we will promote the "Centralization" to the death for the State. In this way, individuals can gain the impression of complete freedom to explore while the legendary burden of personal responsibility will be transferred to the State.

Thus it will be possible to increase dramatically the burden on the State by multiplying, without any limits, the mass of intellectual-functionaries [employed by the state]. Insured, for years in advance, with material security, they are therefore perfect performers of the "Governmental Authority", in other words, our "Power."

Creating an impressive mass of public servants who, alone, will form a Government in the government, regardless of which political party will be in power. This machine can anonymously one day serve as a lever, when the time comes, to accelerate the economic collapse of nation states, because they can not indefinitely sustain such a payroll without having to incur debts beyond their means.

On the other hand, this same machine that will give an image of cold and unresponsive government; this complex machine, useless in many of its functions, will serve as a cover and protection against the people. For who will dare to venture through the mazes of this labyrinth to assert his personal grievances?

Also during this period of general daze, we will also undertake to buy or eliminate, according to the needs of the moment, all business leaders, heads of major state agencies, and the Centres for Scientific Research, whose work and efficiency might give too much power to the Nation-States. It is imperative that the State does not become an independent force in itself, that might escape and endanger our ancestral "Plans".

We will also have an absolute control over all the supranational structures of Nations. These international Bodies should be under our exclusive jurisdiction.

In the same sense, and to ensure the benefit of our influence with the people, we will control all the media information. Our banks will therefore finance only those we favour, while they oversee the closure of the most recalcitrant. This is expected to pass almost unnoticed by the people, who will be absorbed by their need to make more money, and by the entertainment.

We must take care to complete, now, the phased dérégionalisation [sic, ?] of rural areas began at the start of the "Economic Crisis" of 1929. Overcrowd the cities, like during the "Industrial Revolution". The landowners, with their economic independence, and their ability to produce the staple food of the States, are a threat to us, and our future plans. Piled up in cities they are more dependent on our industry to survive.

We cannot allow the existence of independent groups from our "Power". So eliminate landowners by making them slaves to obedient Industries under our control. In regard to the others, we will allow them to organize into Agricultural Cooperatives which our agents will infiltrate to help guide them towards our future priorities.

Using the State, let us highlight the "Respect" due to the, mandatorially diverse, "Cultures", and to the "People", "Religion", and "Ethnicities", which are ways for us to put the concept of "Personal Freedom" before the concept of "National Unity", which will allow us to better divide the populations of Nation States, and thus weaken their authority and their ability to manoeuvre. Taken to extreme limits, but within the international plan, this concept, in the future, will push the ethnic groups of different nations to come together to claim individually its own share of "Power", which will complete the ruin of nations, and will burst into endless wars.

Then the Nation States will be weakened with many battles, all based on the recognition of the "Rights of Minorities" to their independence, the nationalists will be divided into different cultural and religious factions, opposing [each other] blindly in struggles without end, and our youth will have completely lost touch with his roots. So we can then use the UN to begin to impose our New World Order.

Besides, at that stage, the "Humanitarian Ideals, Social and Historical" of the Nation-states, will have long since expired under the pressure of internal divisions.

End of Document 6.6.6. dated at the end of June 1967.

At this point the document from 1967 ends and the one from 1985 begins, as noted here by Serge Monast:

"Eighteen years later, (6.6.6.) in time [meaning that 18 years is 6+6+6], another Reunion of importance was held in Canada. The Group 6.6.6. met again in Toronto, in late June 1985, but this time to finalize the remaining steps that should lead to the collapse of Nation States, and the seizure of International Power through the United Nations."

CHAPTER 2
"The Red Dawn," the 1985 document

Title of the document of 6.6.6.: THE RED DAWN.

The Purpose of the Globalist Project: ESTABLISHMENT OF THE OCCULT WORLD

The Means of Financing the Project: Control of the IMF, GATT, the Commission of Brussels, of NATO, of the UN and other International Organizations.

The last eighteen years were very profitable for the advancement of our global projects. I can tell you, Brothers, we are now touching it, almost there. The fall of Nation-States is only a matter of time, and that rather short, I can tell you with confidence.

With our undercover agents and our colossal financial resources, unprecedented progress has now been made in all areas of Science and Technology, which we control [through] the largest financial corporations. From the secret meetings with Mr. de Rotchild in year 56, and who had intended to finalize the development and global implementation of the "Computer", it is now possible to envisage the establishment of a kind of "International Highway" where all these machines are interconnected. For as you know, direct control of individual people on the planet would be at least totally impossible without the use of computers and their link electronically with respect to each other in a huge "Network World".

These machines also have the advantage in being able to replace millions of people. Moreover, they have neither conscience nor any moral, which is essential for the success of a project like ours. Above all, these machines do, without question, everything that is dictated to them. They are the perfect slaves that have been dreamed by our predecessors, they who were able to suspect that one day it would be possible to accomplish such a prodigy. These machines without a country, no colour, no religion, no political affiliation and achievement, are the ultimate tool for our New World Order. They are the "Cornerstone"!

The organization of these machines into a vast "Network World", which we will control the levers of, we use to immobilize people. How?

As you know, the basic structure of our New World Order is composed, in essence, of a multitude of "Networks", each covering all different spheres of human activity over the whole of the planet. Until now, all these "Networks" were linked together by a common ideological basis: that of man as the "Centre" and "Ultimate Achievement" of the Universe.

So thanks to all these "Networks", united by the bond of the "New Religion of Man to Man", we have easily infiltrated all human sectors in all Western countries, and changed their "Judeo-Christian" basis. The result is that today, this Man, he is part of the Politics, the Economy, the Social, Education, and the Science of Religion, and has already, since our last meeting at the end of June 67, abandoned his past heritage and replaced it with our ideal of a World Religion based solely on Man. Having cut as well as possible its historical roots, this Man is waiting, finally, to be offered a new ideology. This, properly understood, is ours, that of the "Global Village Community", which will be the "Centre". And that is precisely what we will give him, encouraging him to take part, "Body and Soul", in this "Global Electronic Network" where the borders of nation-states have been forever abolished, wiped out up to their deepest roots.

While this lost man will be absorbed by its blind enthusiasm to be part of its new "Global Community", by being part of this vast "Network of Computers", for our part, we shall see, from the levers above, which will be hidden in the file, and be able to identify, to recognize, the rewards of our own goals.

Because within this "New Global Society", any individual with a potential "Profitability" for us, cannot escape. The constant influx of "Electronic Technology" will make sure all the means to file, identify, and monitor all individuals in populations of the West. For those who do not represent "Exploitable Profitability" by ourselves, we will ensure they are eliminated through all the local civil wars that we have taken care to break out here and there through: the work of our servants; and the "Fall of the Economy" of the Nation-States; and the "Oppositions and

Claims" of various groups within those states.

Here is the detail with which we will by 1998 be able to pave the way for the birth of our "World Government":

1. — Expand the "Leisure Society" which has been so profitable to date. By using the invention of the "Video" that we've funded, and games attached to it, end up perverting the morals of youth. Offer him the opportunity now to satisfy all his instincts. A being possessed by his senses, and slave of these, we know, will have neither ideal nor the inner strength to defend anything. It is an "individualist" in nature, and is a perfect candidate which we can easily shape to our desires and our priorities. Besides, remember how easily our predecessors were able to turn all German youth at the beginning of the century using the disillusionment of the latter!

2. — Encourage "Student Causes" for all cases related to the "Ecology". The mandatory protection of the latter will be a major asset on the day we will have pushed the Nation-States to exchange their "Domestic Debt" for a loss of 33% of all their territories remaining in the wild.

3. — Let us fill the inner void of that youth by initiating, from a very young age, the world of computers. Use this as its education system. A slave in the service of another slave we control.

4. — On another level, establish "International Free Trade" as a priority for the economic survival of the Nation-States. This new conception will help us accelerate the economic decline of the "Nationalists" of all nations, to isolate the various factions, and in due course, to fiercely oppose each other in wars that will complete the ruin of these nations.

5. — To ensure at all costs the success of such an endeavour, let us ensure that our agents, who have infiltrated the Ministries of Intergovernmental Affairs and Immigration of the Nation-States,

make major changes to the Statutes of these ministries. These changes will essentially open the doors of immigration to Western countries with a large mass of immigrants entering across their frontiers (immigration that we have indeed caused by having taken care to break out here and there, new localised conflicts). Through well-orchestrated press campaigns targeting public opinion in the Nation-States, we provoke them to accept a large influx of refugees which will have the effect of destabilizing the domestic economy, and increasing racial tensions, in their territory. We will ensure that groups of foreign extremists are part of the influx of immigrants, which will facilitate the political, economic, and social, destabilization of the Nations concerned.

6. – With "Free Trade", which in reality is not free because it is already controlled by us at the top of the economic hierarchy, infiltrated by the"Trilateral Commission" [that of Asia, America and Europe], we will bring discord within the Nation-States by rising unemployment related to restructuring of our Multinationals.

7. – Slowly but surely we will move our multinationals into new countries with the idea of a "Market Economy", such as the countries of Eastern Europe, Russia and China, for example. We do not much care, for the moment, if their population has or has not a large pool of new consumers. What interests us, primarily, is to have access to the "Slave Labour" (cheap and non-union) that we offer these countries and the Third World. Moreover, are their governments not put in place by us? Do they not call for foreign aid and loans from our "International Monetary Fund" and our "World Bank"? Such transfers offer many advantages for us. They help to maintain these new populations in the illusion of an "Economic Liberation", and a "Political Liberty" when in reality we shall prevail over their desire for gain with a debt they can never hope to pay. As for Western populations, they will be maintained in the dream of [Economic Good Times] because products imported from these countries will not suffer any price increase. But on the contrary, without them noticing at first, more and more industries will be forced to close their doors because of

the transfers [of industries] we have made out of Western countries. These closures will increase unemployment and bring significant losses of revenue for the Nation-States.

8. – So we will develop a worldwide "Global Economy" which will completely escape the control of Nation-States. Above all in this new economy, no political or union pressure may have power over her. It will dictate its own "Global Issues" and will require a reorganization of politics, but according to our priorities worldwide.

9. – With this "Economic Independence", having as laws only our laws, we will establish a "Culture of Mass Globalism". By controlling international Television, and Media, we will institute a "New Culture", but levelled, uniform for all, without any future "Creation" escaping us. Artists will reflect our future image or will not survive. No more this time will "Independent Cultural Creations" at any time put in jeopardy our globalist projects, as was so often the case in the past.

10. – By the same economy ["Par cette même économie", ?], we will then be able to make use of the military forces of nation states (such as those in the U.S.) in humanitarian aims. In reality, these "forces" we will use to submit recalcitrant countries to our will. Thus the Third World, and others like them, will not be able to escape our willingness to use their people as slave labour.

11. – To control the world market, we will divert the productivity of its first goal (to free man from the hardness of work). We shall orientate it to turn it against man by enslaving this last to our economic system where he will have no choice but to become our slave, or become a criminal.

12. – All these transfers abroad of our multinationals, and reorganizing the global economy, will aim, inter alia, to drive up unemployment in Western countries. This situation will be more feasible because at the beginning we favoured the massive importation of commodities within the Nation-States, and at the

same time, we have overloaded those States by overuse of their population in the production of services they cannot pay. These extreme conditions will be multiplied by the millions on welfare bodies of all kinds, illiterate, homeless. etc.

13. – With the loss of millions of jobs in the primary sector; caused by the same disguised escape of foreign capital out of the Nation-States, it will be possible to develop the death of social harmony with the spectre of civil war.

14. – The international manipulations of governments and peoples of the Nation-States will give us the excuse to use our IMF to push Western governments to implement "Austerity Budgets", under the cover of a reduction of their illusory "National Debt" and the retaining of their hypothetical "International Credit Rating" and the preservation of the impossible "Social Peace".

15. – Using those "Budgetary Emergency Budgetary Measures", we will break the financing of the Nation-States for all their "Mega-Projects" which represent a direct threat to our global control of the economy.

16. – Besides all these austerity measures will allow us to break the national will in modern structures in the areas of Energy, Agriculture, Transport and New Technologies.

17. – These same measures will give us the perfect opportunity to introduce our "Ideology of Economic Competition". This will mean, within the Nation-States, through the voluntary reduction of wages, the voluntary departure with [the Presentation of Medals for Services rendered], which will open the door to the installation of our "Technology Control". At this time, all departures will be replaced by "Computers" in our service.

18. – These social changes will help us to fundamentally change the workforce and the "Police and Military" of the Nation-States. Without arousing suspicion, under the pretext of the

necessity of time, we will get rid once and for all of all individuals with a "Judeo-Christian Conscience." In this "Restructuring of the Police Corps and the Military" we will dismiss without challenge the older staff, as well as all elements not carrying forward our globalist principles. These will be replaced by young recruits, lacking "Conscience and Morality", and already all trained, and supporting the reckless use of our "Technology of Networked Electronics".

19. – At the same time, and always under the pretext of "budget cuts", we will ensure the transfer of military bases of the Nation-States to the United Nations.

20. – To this end, we will work for the reorganization of the "International Mandate of the UN". From "Peace Force" with no decision making power, we shall raise them to become an "Intervention Force" which will, in a while, render the military forces of the Nation-States homogenous. This will allow us to, without fighting, achieve the demilitarisation of all these states so that none of them in the future are sufficiently strong (independent) to challenge our "World Power".

21. – To accelerate the transfer process, we will involve the current strength of the United Nations in intractable conflicts. In this way, and with the help of the media that we control, we'll show people the impotence and uselessness of this "Force" in its current form. Frustration helping, and pushed to its climax at the right time, it will push the people of Nation-States to beg international bodies to form such a "Multi-National Force" at the earliest opportunity, to protect at all costs the "Peace".

22 . – The emergence of the next global commitment to a "Multi-National Military Force" will go hand in hand with the establishment, within the United Nations, of an "Multi-Jurisdictional Intervention Force". Using this combination of "Effective Police and Military", created by the same pretext of increasing political and social instability within these states collapsing under the burden of economic problems, we can better

control the western populations. Here, the excessive use of electronic filing and identification of individuals will provide a complete monitoring of all populations.

23. – The reorganization of police and military, internal and external, of the Nation-States will converge on the obligation of all to the establishment of a "World Centre of Judiciary". The "Centre" will allow the individual "Police Corps of Nation-States" prompt access to "Databases" on all individuals potentially dangerous to us on the planet. The image of [striving for] better judicial efficiency, and more close links created and maintained with the "Military", will help us highlight the need for an "International Tribunal" coupled with a "Global Justice System", one for civil affairs and criminals, and another for Nations.

24. – During the growing acceptance by all of these new requirements, it will be imperative for us to earlier complete the global control of firearms within the territories of the Nation-States. To do this, we will accelerate the "ALPHA PLAN" implemented during the 60s by some of our predecessors. This "Plan" originally had two objectives which have remained the same today:
– through the intervention of "crazy shooters" creating a climate of insecurity in people to get them to [support] tighter control of firearms.
– orient violence so as to put the blame on religious extremists, or people with religious affiliations who tend to the "Traditional" or, of persons claiming to have privileged communications with God.
Today, to accelerate the "Control of Firearms," we can use the "Collapse of Economic Conditions" of the Nation-States which will take with it a complete destabilization of the Social [fabric], so increasing violence. I needn't need to remind you or show you, Brothers, the foundations of this "Control" of firearms. Without it, it would become almost impossible for us to make kneel down the populations of those targeted States. Remember how well our predecessors were able to control Germany in 1930 with the new

"laws" implemented at the time, laws which are now the foundation of the current laws of Nation-States for the same control.

25. – These "Steps" refer to the "OMEGA PHASE" experienced from experiments conducted in the early 70s. They contain the application, globally, of "Electro-Magnetic Weapons." The "Changes of Climate" has caused the:
– destruction of crops, and failure, under these conditions, of agricultural land;
– denaturation, by artificial means, of food products of common consumption;
– the poisoning of nature by an excessive, indiscriminate and widespread use of chemicals in agriculture;
and all this, Brothers, this will lead to certain ruin the food industries of the Nation-States. The future of "Population Control" of these states must go [hand in hand] with the absolute control by us of food production globally, and by taking control of the main "Food Routes" ["Routes Alimentaires", agricultural regions?] in the world. For this, it is necessary to use the Electro-Magnetic, among others, to destabilize the climates of the States most productive agriculturally. As to the poisoning of nature, it will be speeded up all the more as the increase of populations will push it without restriction.

26. – The use of the Electro-Magnetic will cause "Earthquakes" in the most important industrial regions of the Nation-States, to help speed up the "Economic Collapse" of States most threatening to us; as well to amplify the obligation of the establishment of our New World Order [sic, meaning presumably a kind of global blackmail].

27. – Who will we suspect? Who could have suspected the use of these means? Those who dare against us by disseminating information about the existence and content of our "conspiracy", will become suspect in the eyes of the authorities of their nation and their people. Thanks to the misinformation, lies, hypocrisy, and individualism, that we have created among the people of the

Nation-States, this Man will become an enemy for humans. Thus these "Independent Individuals", who are more dangerous to us precisely because of their "Freedom", will be considered by their peers as enemies, not liberators. Child slavery, the pillaging of the Third World, unemployment, propaganda for the liberalisation of anti-drug laws, the brutalization of the youth of Nations, the ideology of "Respect for Individual Freedom" diffused in Judeo-Christian Churches and within the Nation-States, obscurantism considered as a basis of pride, inter-ethnic conflicts, and our latest achievement: "Budget cuts"; with all that we can finally see the performance of our ancestral "Dream": the introduction of our "NEW WORLD ORDER".

End of Document of the End of June 1985.

CONCLUSION
by Serge Monast

So, the "PROTOCOL OF TORONTO (6.6.6.)", myth or reality? It would be like asking if "The Brave New World" is also a myth or reality even if it is a novel. For its author also had access to "Documents" of the period to create it. Its author knew that the disclosure, the dissemination of information that he possessed, in a different form than the novel, would have awakened in people a lot more distrust than acceptance. And how many other authors had used the same ploy to warn their contemporaries and future generations?

So, the "PROTOCOL OF TORONTO (6.6.6.)", myth or reality?

The urgency of the actual situation, that generated by the start the "Budgetary Limitations" which marks the beginning of the end, close to the realisation of the "Occult New World Order", allows not the writing of a novel (which would have taken too much time in the present context).

But the impact caused by the revelation of the "Documents" is still important because when they are published it will effectively put on the defensive those who are behind them.

What is desired, here, is that beyond the misinformation conveyed, and maintained by unscrupulous politicians and by people frightened about the possibility of losing self interest, each reader can reflect, together with others like him, and now take means to survive in the face of what comes.

Even though my life is in danger because of the dissemination of this information to you, yours is even more so due to your ignorance of the same information.

So, the "PROTOCOL OF TORONTO (6.6.6.)", myth or reality?

It is for you to answer ...

For you to see in the recent past and future events, if these "documents" belong to the realm of fiction or reality.

For you to realize that fear has no other purpose than to paralyse you and put you to thank those who want to control you, to better enslave you according to their interests, which are ultimately, not yours.

So, the "PROTOCOL OF TORONTO (6.6.6.)", myth or reality?

Serge Monast / Investigative Reporter / at the End of March 1995."

Serge Monast (1945-1996) died a year after releasing this document from a heart attack suffered in suspicious circumstances only a day after he was released from jail.

If you liked this book you might like to read some of the author's other works, including:

In Defence of Conspiracy Theories
This book is an attempt to address the widespread criticism of 'conspiracy theories', raising issues like: the control and negligence of the main organs of the media and police which make it difficult for true information to reach the public (and hence the public remain in ignorance of – and dismiss as a 'conspiracy theory' – the true facts); and the public's habit of underestimating the complexity of modern day politics. A number of complex political plots and allegations are described in detail including: the 1641 Rebellion, British Intelligence manipulation of the 1919-21 Irish leaders, Secret Societies and the role of Occult organisations in Ireland and around the world, the allegations that Martin McGuinness is a British agent, and the motivation behind large scale immigration into Ireland. The author also addresses the question of value systems in modern Western societies and asks are even these being manipulated in order to assist the process of political control.
978-0-9556812-2-6

Orwellian Ireland
Inspired by the book Stasiland, this work is an attempt to see if some of the state practices that flourished in Communist Eastern Europe might be replicated in modern Ireland. It goes into the question of intelligence agencies, what agencies are active in Ireland, how they harass dissidents, their use of modern technology and their role in secretly supporting paramilitary groups in Ireland and around the world. It includes a lot of first hand testimony of state harassment, and even torture, which is on a par with what happened in countries like East Germany. Finally it concludes with some searching questions about the real government policies being pursued in Ireland.
978-0-9556812-0-2

Shakespeare was Irish!
As more and more scholars come to realise that the accepted story of William Shakespeare is untenable, this book tries to unmask the covert Irish influence on his work and the remarkable career of William Nugent, the only Irish candidate ever put forward for Shakespeare. It includes the full text of many original documents on Irish history, from the Reformation to the 1641 Rebellion.

'That in these lines I could as well express,
As in my soul I do admire her beauty,
Or that great Daniel, fit for such a task,
This wonder of our Isle, had seen, and heeded,
Then should his glorious muse, her worth unmask,
And he himself, himself should have exceeded;
Then England, France, Spain, Greece and Italy,
And all that th'Ocean from our shores divideth,

Would over-run their bounds, and hither fly,
To find the treasure, that our Ireland hideth,
But best is, that we never do disclose it,
Since known but of ourselves, we shall not lose it.'
- Richard Nugent, *Cynthia* (London, 1604)
978-0-9556812-1-9

An Creideam

This book seeks to illustrate the type of literature that shaped and influenced the Irish people's faith over the centuries. It is intended as a cornucopia of Catholic writing, a skirl around the kind of books and journals that graced Irish priest's libraries over the years. Outlined in chronological order it gives the full text of the Confession of St. Patrick, the Life of St. Columbanus, an ancient Irish tract on the mass; extracts from the Confessions of St. Augustine, the Irish Annals, and the fiction of Canon Sheehan; some theology from St. Thomas Aquinas, from 'A Handbook of Moral Theology', and the doctrine of Purgatory from an old Maynooth theologian; historical or contemporary accounts from all centuries, all the way from Tertullian, through Lough Derg in the 15th century, the Cromwellian Wars of the 17th century, to the social and economic teachings of the Church in the 19th and early 20th centuries.
978-0-9556812-3-3

Slí na Fírinne

This English language book puts the traditional Catholic proofs of God's existence into a modern context. It covers most of the arguments raging in the theism v atheism debate and also includes quotes on the nature of God and his existence from c.80 philosophers and scientists.
978-0-9556812-8-8

The Irish Invented Chess!

For over three centuries a controversy has raged as to the exact origins of 'fidchell' – in modern Irish 'ficheall' – or Irish chess, a game played in Ireland from biblical times. This book argues that that game of fidchell, or brannaimh, was recognisably our modern chess. It also raises disturbing questions about the real history surrounding the Lewis Chess find.
978-0-9556812-6-4

www.ingramcontent.com/pod-product-compliance
Lightning Source LLC
Chambersburg PA
CBHW020959180526
45163CB00006B/2429